How People Lived

How People Lived in
Ancient
Egypt

Jane Bingham

PowerKiDS
press™
New York

Published in 2009 by The Rosen Publishing Group Inc.
29 East 21st Street, New York, NY 10010

First Edition

Library of Congress Cataloging-in-Publication Data

Bingham, Jane.
  How people lived in ancient Egypt / Jane Bingham. — 1st ed.
      p. cm. — (How people lived)
  Includes index.
  ISBN 978-1-4042-4433-7 (library binding)
  ISBN 978-1-4358-2623-6 (paperback)
  ISBN 978-1-4358-2637-3 (6-pack)
 1. Egypt—Social life and customs—To 332 B.C.—Juvenile literature. I. Title.
  DT61.B539 2009
  932—dc22

                                    2007040193

Cover (main image): Queen Nerfertiti was the chief wife of Pharaoh Akhaten and the mother of
daughters. Here she wears a simple crown and a wide, bead necklace.

Picture acknowledgments: ARPL/HIP/Topfoto: 11; The Art Archive/Corbis: 3, 18; Bettmann/Corb
7; The British Library/HIP/Topfoto: 10, 14; The British Museum/Werner Forman Archive: 19; The
British Museum/HIP/Topfoto: front cover tl & bl, 5, 13, 15, 24, 25; The Egyptian Museum,
Cairo/Werner Forman Archive: 16; Werner Forman Archive: 26; Werner Forman Archive/Corbis:
12; Historical Picture Archive/Corbis: 22; Gianni Dagli Orti/Corbis: 17; Ronald Sheridan/AAAC: 2
Spectrum Colour Library/HIP/Topfoto:front cover cl, 9; Topfoto: 27; Charles Walker/Topfoto: fro
cover main, 23; Ron Watts/Corbis: 21; Roger Wood/Corbis: 8.

Map by Peter Bull.

Manufactured in China

CONTENTS

Words that appear in **bold**
can be found in the glossary
on page 28.

WHO WERE THE ANCIENT EGYPTIANS?

▲ A map of Ancient Egypt, showing the main cities. (Modern names shown in parentheses.)

The Ancient Egyptians began as a race of people who lived on the banks of the River Nile, in North Africa. Gradually, they learned how to grow crops and irrigate the land, and by 5000 B.C., they were farming the fertile soil beside the river. The farmers settled in villages, which in time, grew into larger communities.

EGYPT UNITES

By the fourth century B.C., there were two kingdoms on the River Nile: Upper Egypt and Lower Egypt. Then, around 3100 B.C., the kingdoms were united by **Pharaoh** Menes. He built a capital city at Memphis, and started a **dynasty** (or family) of powerful rulers.

THREE PERIODS

The Ancient Egyptian **civilization** lasted for over 2000 years. Historians have identified three great periods in this long history. The Old Kingdom (ca. 2575–2150 B.C.) was the time when most of the great pyramids were built. The Middle Kingdom (ca. 1975–1640 B.C.) was the period when art and literature flourished. The New Kingdom (ca. 1539–1075 B.C.) was a time of expansion, when the Egyptians gained an empire that was at its largest in about 1450 B.C.

EYGPTIAN TIMELINE

5000 B.C.	4000	3000

ca. 5000 B.C. Farming begins in the Nile valley.

ca. 3100 B.C. Pharaoh Menes unites Upper and Lower Egypt.

ca. 2575 B.C. Old Kingdom begins.

THE END OF THE EMPIRE

the first century B.C., the Egyptian
mpire had started to weaken and the
yptians had to defend themselves
ainst many enemies. Finally, in 332 B.C.,
ey were conquered by a Greek army led
Alexander the Great. For the next 300
ars, Egypt was ruled by members of the

Ptolemy family, who were descended
from one of Alexander's **generals**.

In 32 B.C., Rome went to war with Egypt.
The Egyptians were defeated and their
ruler, Queen Cleopatra, killed herself.
Egypt became part of the Roman Empire
in 30 B.C., and the great Egyptian
civilization came to an end.

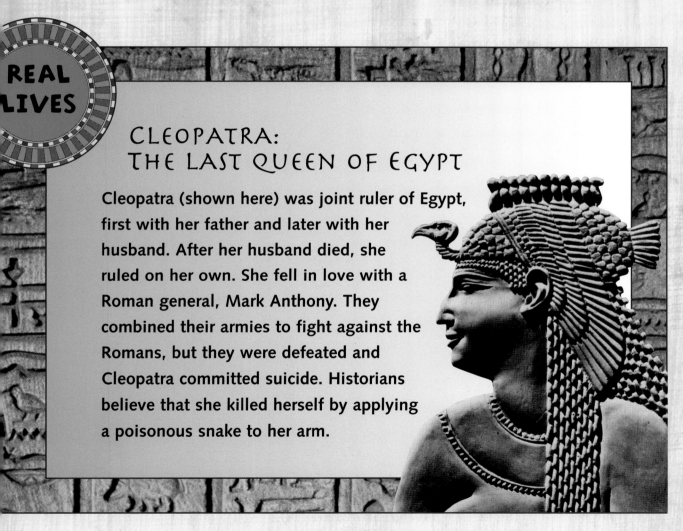

REAL LIVES

CLEOPATRA: THE LAST QUEEN OF EGYPT

Cleopatra (shown here) was joint ruler of Egypt,
first with her father and later with her
husband. After her husband died, she
ruled on her own. She fell in love with a
Roman general, Mark Anthony. They
combined their armies to fight against the
Romans, but they were defeated and
Cleopatra committed suicide. Historians
believe that she killed herself by applying
a poisonous snake to her arm.

2000   1000   0

1975 B.C. Middle
ngdom begins.

ca. 1539 B.C. New
Kingdom begins.

ca. 1450 B.C. Egyptian
Empire at its largest.

332 B.C. Alexander
the Great conquers
Egypt.

30 B.C. Egypt becomes
part of the Roman Empire.

EGYPTIAN MEN, WOMEN, AND CHILDREN

Ancient Egyptian society was divided into two main classes: the wealthy rulers and nobles, and the ordinary working people. Men of all classes had more freedom than women, but Egyptian women had more rights than women in Ancient Greece and Rome.

EGYPTIAN MEN

Egyptian men saw themselves as the head of the household, but most of them left the job of running the home to their wives. By law, men could have as many wives as they wished, and some pharaohs had hundreds. However, most Egyptians could only afford to support one wife.

EGYPTIAN WOMEN

Women in Ancient Egypt had the right to own property and to run a business. If an Egyptian woman was accused of a crime, she could appear in court to defend herself.

Wealthy women had a large staff of servants to help them run their homes, but women from poor families did all the housework themselves, with the help of their daughters. Only a few noblewomen went out to work, but poorer women often helped their husbands in the fields, or did other jobs in the community (see pages 18–21). Egyptian women of all classes were kept very busy bringing up

▲ The most important person in Ancient Egypt was the pharaoh, or king. Ancient Egyptian pharaohs were treated like gods by their people. This painting shows Pharaoh Ramses III embracing the goddess Isis.

their families. It was not unusual for a woman to give birth to ten children, although it was rare for all the children to survive.

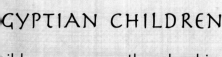

EGYPTIAN CHILDREN

Children were greatly valued in Egyptian society and most children enjoyed a close family life. However, by the time they were 12 years old, Egyptian children were seen as adults. Girls could be married at this age, and the children from poorer families were expected to start full-time work. Some Egyptian children started to work with their parents before they were even five years old.

◄ An Egyptian carving of a husband and wife. The couple seem to be fond of each other, since the wife has her arm around her husband's shoulders. The two small figures are probably their children.

REAL LIVES

NAUNAKTE: A NOBLEWOMAN

An Egyptian noblewoman, known simply as Lady Naunakte, wrote a will before she died. Naunakte obviously had property and wealth of her own, independently of her husband. In her will, she proudly announced that she had managed to provide for all her children. Naunakte wrote, "I am a free woman of Egypt. I have raised eight children, and have provided them with everything suitable for their station in life."

WHO WAS IN CHARGE IN ANCIENT EGYPTIAN TIMES?

At the head of Egyptian society was the all-powerful pharaoh. He made all the important decisions about how his kingdom was run. Ministers helped to rule Egypt, and hundreds of officials ran the different regions of the Empire.

POWERFUL PHARAOHS

There were a few examples of powerful female pharaohs, but pharaohs in Ancient Egypt were almost always male. The pharaoh lived in a vast palace with his many wives and children. All the members of the royal family were treated with great respect, but the most important person, after the pharaoh, was his chief wife. The pharaoh usually chose one of his sisters to be his chief wife and her son became the next pharaoh. This way, the divine blood of pharaohs remained as "pure" as possible.

As well as ruling their kingdom, pharao[h] also led the Egyptian army. One of the greatest warrior pharaohs was Tuthmos[is] III, who conquered more than 300 citie[s] and led his army to war 17 times over [a] period of 25 years. Pharaohs gave orde[rs] for magnificent monuments to be built. Teams of builders constructed huge pyramids and temples in honor of the pharaohs.

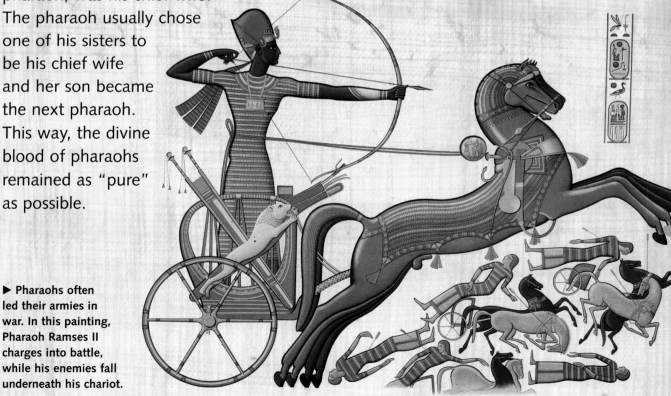

▶ Pharaohs often led their armies in war. In this painting, Pharaoh Ramses II charges into battle, while his enemies fall underneath his chariot.

VIZIERS AND VICEROYS

ree important ministers helped the
araoh to run Egypt. Two **viziers** were in
arge of Upper and Lower Egypt, and a
ceroy governed Nubia (a large territory
the south of Egypt). These three men
d a large staff of officials who collected
xes, ran the law courts, and supervised
rming and building projects.

GENERALS AND PRIESTS

Army generals had a lot of power in
Ancient Egypt. A few very talented
generals even became pharaohs
themselves. High priests were also very
powerful figures. It was believed that
they could interpret the will of the gods,
and so they were often asked to advise
the pharaoh.

REAL LIVES

TUTANKHAMUN: A BOY PHARAOH

Tutankhamun was the son of Pharaoh
Akhenaten. When he was about nine
years old, his father died, so
Tutankhamun became pharaoh. Around
this time he was married to his half-
sister Ankhesenamun, who was slightly
older than him. Because Tutankhamun
was so young, two adult regents ruled
for him. He died when he was about 19,
probably from a broken leg that became
infected. Tutankhamun's mummified body
was preserved inside a magnificent set of coffin
cases, one of which is shown here.

WHAT WAS LIFE LIKE IN AN EGYPTIAN FAMILY?

Most Egyptian families were much larger than families today. An Egyptian household usually consisted of an older married couple and their sons, who each had their own wife and children. Wealthy families also had servants to help them run their home. In addition to all these people, there were often animals running around the house: cats, dogs, and monkeys were popular family pets.

FAMILY HOMES

Rich Egyptians lived in large villas with many rooms and a central hall for entertaining guests. The rooms were furnished with wooden tables, chairs, and beds. Villas often had shady yards and pools, and were sometimes surrounded by their own farming lands.

Ordinary families had simple cottages with just a few rooms. The same room was used for eating and sleeping, and benches around the sides of the room could be used as seats or beds.

▲ Wealthy Egyptian families often lived in villas surrounded by farmland. This painting shows servants at work in a villa and on its farm.

USBANDS AND WIVES

yptian girls were usually married in their early
ens. Boys often waited to marry until they were
ound 20 years old and they had become established
their work. Divorce was easy in Egyptian society—
th partners had the right to ask the courts to end a
rriage. However, there is evidence that most
uples stayed together for life.

AMILY SERVANTS

h people kept a large staff of servants to help them
their villas and the surrounding lands. Within the
me, servants cooked and cleaned and repaired the
nily's clothes. They also waited on their master and
stress, and helped to care for the children.

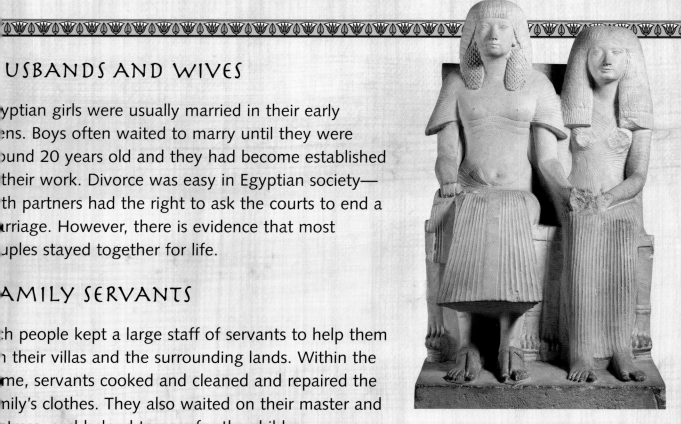

▲ A young Egyptian couple from the ruling class.
The couple share a carved throne, and they are
finely dressed in pleated robes and heavy wigs.

REAL LIVES

MEKET-RE: A VILLA OWNER

Meket-Re was an important Egyptian official who lived in the
third century B.C. His tomb contains painted wooden models of
his family home with its gardens and pool, and also its
kitchens, workshops, and grain stores. One set of models
shows Meket-Re with his son and four scribes, counting the
cattle on his estate. The models provide a fascinating picture of
the home life of a leading member of the Egyptian ruling class.

BABIES AND YOUNG CHILDREN

In Ancient Egypt, one in five children died before they reached their teens, so people did everything they could to keep them safe. Parents tried to protect their children with prayers and spells, and babies and children wore amulets (lucky charms) around their neck.

Mothers from ordinary families cared fo their own children, often breast-feeding them until they were three years old. Wealthy women paid poorer mothers to do the job of breast-feeding their babie

BOYS AND GIRLS

From an early age, boys and girls were kept apart. Wealthy boys learned how read and write. Boys from ordinary families trained to do the same work as their father. A son might work beside father in the fields, or learn the famil trade in a workshop.

Girls of all classes stayed at hor with their mothers. Wealthy girls learned how to run a household and supervise slaves Girls from poor families were expected to help look after the younger sisters and brothers. They also learned how to cook and clean, and how to spin and weave cloth to make the family's clothes.

◀ A pharaoh and his teacher. This painting shows a young ruler sitting on the lap of hi female tutor. Wealthy Egyptians were often taught at home.

CHILDREN'S TOYS

Young children played with wooden balls, dolls, and spinning tops. They also had model animals made from clay or wood. Some of these animals had moving parts that were worked by pulling a string.

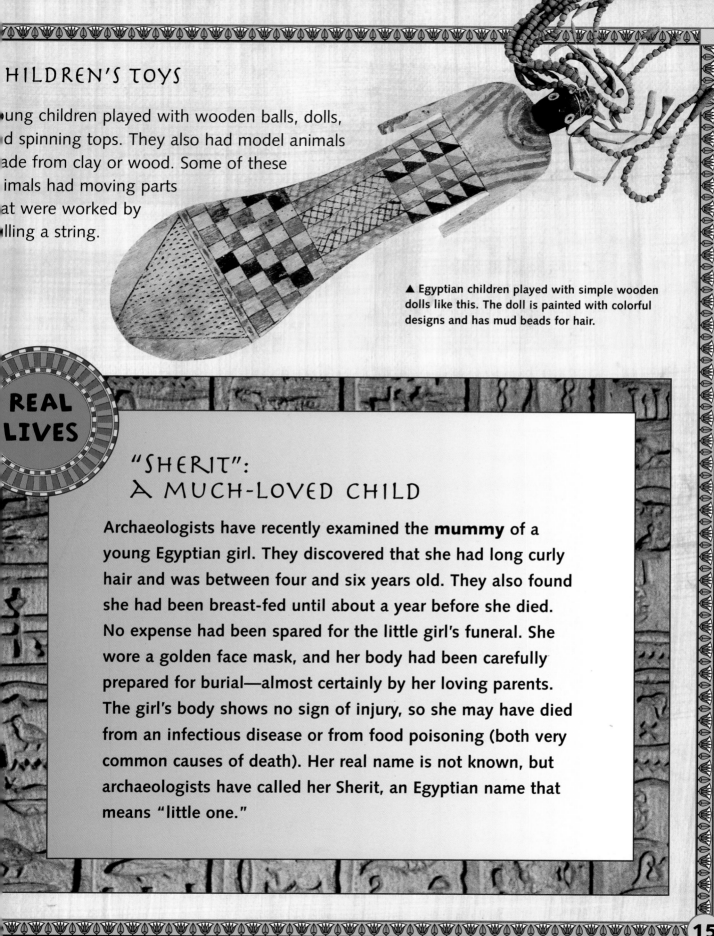

▲ Egyptian children played with simple wooden dolls like this. The doll is painted with colorful designs and has mud beads for hair.

REAL LIVES

"SHERIT": A MUCH-LOVED CHILD

Archaeologists have recently examined the **mummy** of a young Egyptian girl. They discovered that she had long curly hair and was between four and six years old. They also found she had been breast-fed until about a year before she died. No expense had been spared for the little girl's funeral. She wore a golden face mask, and her body had been carefully prepared for burial—almost certainly by her loving parents. The girl's body shows no sign of injury, so she may have died from an infectious disease or from food poisoning (both very common causes of death). Her real name is not known, but archaeologists have called her Sherit, an Egyptian name that means "little one."

DID EGYPTIAN CHILDREN GO TO SCHOOL?

Most Egyptian children did not go to school. Children in poor families had to help their parents with their work, and rich boys and girls often had a private tutor to teach them at home. However, there were some schools attached to the temples, although they only took boys.

TEMPLE SCHOOLS

Some temple schools were attached to important temples in the cities, and only took boys from the ruling classes. There were also smaller temple schools in the villages. The village schools were open to all boys, but they were expensive, so families had to save up to send their sons to school.

Boys started at temple school when they were around five years old. For the first few years, they concentrated on copying texts and reading aloud. The teachers at the temple schools were very strict, and pupils were often beaten for not working hard enough.

Older pupils studied more advanced texts, such as the *Book of Wisdom*, which gave advice to young men on how to behave. Later, some students specialized in different subjects, such as mathematics, religion, engineering, and medicine.

▲ The Ancient Egyptians did not have an alphabet. Instead, they used a system of picture signs—known as hieroglyphs—write things down. The hieroglyphs shown here were painted on a coffin.

GYPTIAN WRITING

yptian writing was very hard to learn,
cause it was made up of more than 700
ture signs called hieroglyphs. Some of the
eroglyphs represent an object or a
rson. Others represent a sound.

hool pupils wrote with a reed pen
ped in ink. They practiced their writing
pieces of broken pottery or flakes of
ne that could be thrown away. By the
d of their schooling, they were ready to
write on **papyrus**—a kind of fine, white
paper made from reeds.

SCRIBES

Many pupils at temple schools later became
scribes. This was a very important job, and
scribes had a high position in Egyptian society.
They kept all the records needed to run the
kingdom of Egypt. They also wrote the
histories of the pharaohs and their deeds.

▼ A carving of the scribe Amenhotep at work. Amenhotep
sits cross-legged to write on his scroll, using his stretched-
out kilt as a desk.

REAL LIVES

AMENHOTEP: A ROYAL SCRIBE

Amenhotep was a very well-
educated man. He was the special
scribe of Pharaoh Amenhotep III,
but also an architect, priest,
teacher, and healer. He drew
up the plans for the pharaoh's
massive building projects and
organized their construction.
After his death, he became
famous for his teachings.
Amenhotep was eventually
worshipped as a god of healing.

WHAT JOBS DID EGYPTIAN PEOPLE DO?

Most Egyptians were farmers on the banks of the River Nile. Many others worked as fishermen, weavers, or potters. Educated people had jobs as government officials, priests, scribes, and doctors. Merchants made long journeys to exchange goods, and men of all classes joined the army.

WOMEN'S WORK

Most Egyptian women stayed at home, but a few had careers. Noblewomen could become priestesses. They could also work as singers, dancers, and musicians in the temples. Poorer women had jobs as weavers in workshops, or as servants to the rich. Women from farming families worked with the men in the fields.

▼ Egyptian couples often worked together in the fields. Here, the husband plows the earth and scares away the birds, while his wife follows, sowing seeds.

SLAVE LABOR

By the time of the New Kingdom, slaver was common. Many slaves were prisone of war from the lands that the Egyptian had won for their Empire (see pages 6–7 They were often employed as builders, miners, or household servants. Some sla had very hard lives, but others were we treated. A few slaves were set free and some of them married local people.

WORKING ON THE LAND

Egyptian farmers grew a variety of vegetables, figs, dates, and grapes, but their main crop was wheat. Most the land was used for crops but farmers also kept some animals, such as sheep, pigs goats, geese, and ducks. Ox were used as working anima and only rich farmers reared cows to eat.

CRAFTSPEOPLE

Skilled Egyptian craftspeople produced a wide variety of goods. Potters worked with clay, or carved pots from stone, and carpenters used local and imported woods to make furniture and statues. Metalworkers made tools and weapons, and jewellers created elaborate pieces from silver and gold, beads and precious stones. Craftspeople sometimes worked in a family group, or as part of a team in a large workshop.

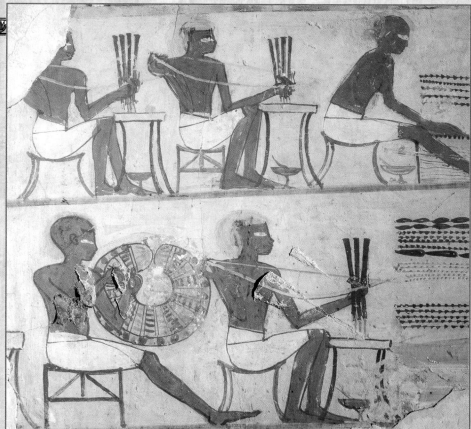

▲ This painting shows a jewelry workshop. The workers are boring holes in beads, polishing the beads, and threading them on a wide collar.

ASRU: A SINGER

A coffin has survived from Ancient Egypt that contains the mummified body of a working woman. The coffin inscription says that she was Asru, a singer in a temple. Archaeologists believe Asru was at least 60 when she died. This was unusual in Egyptian times, when most women did not survive beyond 40. Asru's long life was probably due to the fact that she had a safe and comfortable life working in a temple.

BUILDING TEMPLES AND PYRAMIDS

Thousands of Egyptians worked on the massive pyramids and temples of Ancient Egypt. Miners cut stone from quarries, and stonecutters shaped it into blocks. Then teams of workers hauled the blocks onto sleds and took them to where they were needed. Builders set the massive stones in place and masons trimmed them to fit.

ARMY LIFE

By the time of the New Kingdom, Egypt had a large professional army. The ordinary soldiers came from the lower classes, but officers were always educated, wealthy men. Life in the Egyptian army was tough. Soldiers were sent on long marches and had to train very hard. Egyptian soldiers carried spears and shields, but they had no protective armor, so they suffered terrible injuries.

DOCTORS

Egyptian doctors were famous throughout the Middle East for their skill. They studied medical texts and specialized in different areas of the body, such as the stomach, the teeth, or the head. Doctors performed surgery, sewed up cuts, set broken limbs, and treated wounds. They also made medicines from plants and **minerals** and even animal parts. If these methods failed to work, doctors also tried to use spells and magic charms to help them cure their patients.

▼ This painting shows workmen pulling blocks of stone on a sled. The man at the back of the group is probably the foreman, who gave orders to the workers.

preserved the bodies as **mummies**. The people who did this important work were known as **embalmers**. They worked in tents beside the River Nile.

Embalmers prepared the bodies of the dead for burial. First, they removed the brains and **internal organs** and stored them in jars. Then they covered the body with a salt called natron to help it dry out. When the body was thoroughly dry, its insides were stuffed with a mixture of linen, sawdust, and sweet-smelling spices. Finally, the embalmers wrapped the mummy in layers of bandages, and placed it in a coffin, ready to be buried in a tomb.

MBALMERS

e Egyptians believed in life after death. ey thought that the dead would need eir bodies in the **next world**, so they

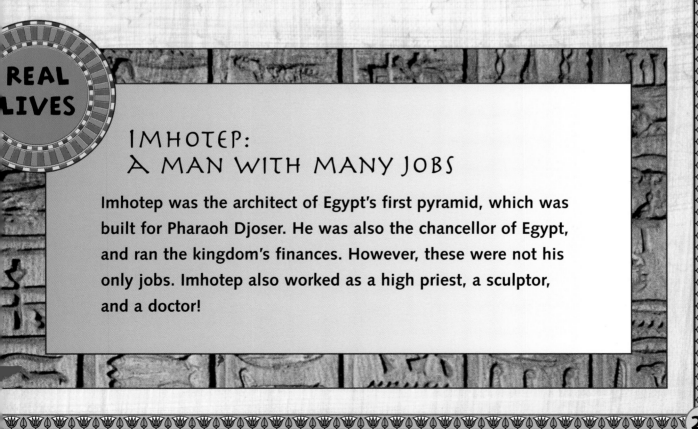

REAL LIVES

IMHOTEP: A MAN WITH MANY JOBS

Imhotep was the architect of Egypt's first pyramid, which was built for Pharaoh Djoser. He was also the chancellor of Egypt, and ran the kingdom's finances. However, these were not his only jobs. Imhotep also worked as a high priest, a sculptor, and a doctor!

What did Egyptian adults and children wear?

In the hot, dry climate of Ancient Egypt people did not need many clothes. In fact, most children went naked until they were in their teens. Most Egyptians wore simple clothes, but added a lot of jewelry to make themselves look good.

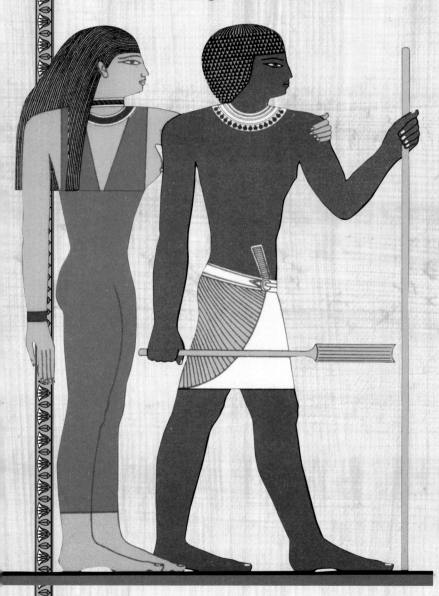

▲ Most Egyptians dressed very simply, in kilts for the men and long tunic-dresses for the women. Women's tunics were usually white, but sometimes they were dyed dramatic colors.

Changing styles

Until the time of the New Kingdom, all the Egyptians wore the same basic clothes. Men wore a simple kilt, made from a piece of linen wrapped around the waist. Women wore a long tunic that reached their ankles. Wealthy people's clothes were made from fine linen, but ordinary people used a thicker, coarser cloth. People of all classes wore sandals made from reeds.

In the New Kingdom, styles changed. Fashionable people wore cloaks made from very thin, pleated linen. Some men wore a double kilt (one long and one short), and women's tunics were decorated with ornaments and fringes.

Looking good

Rich men and women spent a lot of time on their looks. They bathed every day and rubbed scented oils on their skin. Both sexes wore heavy eye makeup. They believed that it protected their eyes from the glare of the sun and prevented eye

sease. For special occasions, men and
omen wore heavy wigs, decorated with
eads and jewels.

l Egyptians liked to wear jewelry, and
oth men and women wore necklaces,
acelets, and earrings. Wealthy people
ore jewelry made from gold and
ecious stones. Poor people's jewelry
as made from copper and beads.

▶ A carving of the elegant Queen Nefertiti.
Here, the queen wears a simple crown and
a wide, bead necklace.

A SPECIAL HAIRSTYLE

Egyptian children had their own special
hairstyle. Their hair was shaved off or
kept very short except for a lock on the
side of the head. This long, s-shaped curl
was called the "side-lock of youth."
Children wore this style until they were
around 12 years old, when they were
considered to be adults.

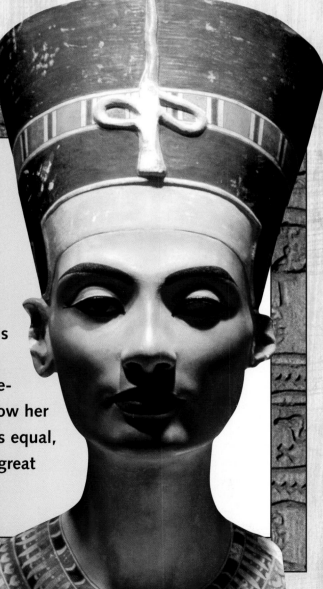

REAL
LIVES

NEFERTITI:
A BEAUTIFUL
QUEEN

Nefertiti was the chief wife of
Pharaoh Akhaten and the mother
of six daughters. In carvings, she is
shown as very beautiful, with a
long, slim neck and carefully made-
up eyes and lips. Some carvers show her
standing beside the pharaoh as his equal,
and this probably means she had great
influence over her husband.

HOW DID EGYPTIAN ADULTS AND CHILDREN HAVE FUN?

People in Ancient Egypt really liked to enjoy themselves. Wealthy Egyptians held lavish banquets, with music and dancing. Kings and nobles hunted as a sport, and people of all classes played sports and games.

EGYPTIAN PARTIES

Rich Egyptians held large parties. They provided banquets with many courses and plenty of entertainments. During the feast, musicians played on harps, flutes, pipes, and drums. Later in the evening, singers, dancers, jugglers, and acrobats entertained the guests.

HUNTING AND FISHING

Hunting and fishing were popular sports for wealthy Egyptians. Nobles hunted water birds on the banks of the Nile, and rode on chariots into the desert to hunt for lions, ostriches, and cobras. Sometime hunters formed a team to spear a hippo and catch it in a net. Other noblemen preferred to stay at home and fish in the own private pools.

▶ In this painting of a banquet, servant girls dance for the guests and serve them food. Servants also placed cones of perfumed fat on the guests' heads. The cones gradually melted, creating a sweet smell.

SPORTS AND GAMES

The Egyptians loved to compete against each other in athletic contests. Ancient Egyptian sports included boxing, gymnastics, running, rowing, jumping, and throwing the javelin. People played a kind of hockey, using palm tree branches as sticks and a leather ball stuffed with papyrus. They also formed teams for energetic tug-of-war games, in which each team pulled as hard as they could to show they were the strongest.

When they were not playing sports, Egyptians of all ages liked to relax at home with a board game. One of the most popular games was "senet." It had a set of pieces that were moved across a board, much like the modern game of backgammon.

REAL LIVES

NEBAMUN: A NOBLE WHO LOVED TO HUNT

Nebamun was a nobleman who died around 1400 B.C. In a painting in his tomb (shown here), he is pictured hunting for birds in the marshes of the River Nile. Nebamun is shown holding a throwing stick, which was used to stun the birds. Also in the painting are his wife and daughter, and his handsome ginger-colored cat. Nebamun's cat would have been specially trained to frighten the birds from their hiding place.

HOW IMPORTANT WAS RELIGION FOR THE EGYPTIANS?

The Ancient Egyptians worshipped dozens of gods and goddesses. Every village had its own shrine, where people could say prayers and leave offerings to the gods. There were also massive temples on the banks of the Nile. On feast days, priests carried statues of the gods around towns and cities, and people sang songs and prayed. Then the priests sacrificed animals to the gods.

▲ This carving shows a man presenting an offering to a sacred bull. Behind the bull stands the goddess Isis.

TALKING TO THE GODS

Everybody in Ancient Egypt tried to follow the will of the gods. If they had to make a big decision in their lives, they paid a scribe to write down their question for the god. This request was handed to a priest, who disappeared into the temple and returned with an answer. Then the grateful people left a gift of thanks to the gods.

PREPARING FOR THE NEXT WORLD

The Egyptians believed that after they died, they would go to the next world to live with the gods. This belief led them to bury the dead with great care (see page 21). Embalmers preserved the bodies of people of all classes and even favorite pets. People were often buried with their possessions, so that they would have everything they needed in the next world

ERVANTS OF THE GODS

me men and women devoted their
es to the gods. Women often
orked as musicians and dancers in
e temples. Male priests conducted
emonies and wrote sacred texts.
me priests and priestesses worked in
ge temples, which contained a
tue of a god or goddess. Every
orning, they "woke" the statue.
en they washed and dressed it,
ered it food, and prayed to it.

Pharaoh Ramses II built two magnificent temples at
u Simbel in honor of the gods. These four giant
ures carved from the rock represent Ramses and
ee other gods.

REAL
LIVES

THUYA:
A PRIESTESS

**Thuya was the high priestess of the rain god, Min. She was
married to Yuya, the high priest of Min. The couple were
important people at the court of Pharaoh Amenhotep III. (Yuya
was in charge of the royal chariots.) Later, their daughter Tiy
became Queen of Egypt. Thuya's golden mummy case shows
a round-faced woman with a very contented smile.**

Glossary

archaeologist Someone who learns about the past by examining old buildings and objects.

chancellor The person in charge of a country's money.

civilization A well-organized society.

dynasty A ruling family.

embalmer Someone who prepares the bodies of the dead for burial.

fertile Good for growing crops.

general A leader of soldiers in an army.

hieroglyph A picture or a symbol that represents an object, a letter, or a sound.

high priest/ priestess A very important man/woman priest.

inscription A carved message, often on a tomb.

internal organs Body parts, such as the heart or the stomach, that are on the inside of the body.

irrigate To supply water to crops.

mineral A substance, such as iron and salt, which is found under the earth.

minister Someone in charge of a government department.

mummy A body that has been specially treated and then wrapped in bandages, to stop it from decaying.

next world A place where the dead go after their life on Earth, according to Ancient Egyptian beliefs.

official Someone who holds an important position in a government.

papyrus A kind of paper made from a reedlike plant.

pharaoh An Egyptian kin◦

regent Someone who rul◦ on behalf of the real ruler ◦ a country.

sacrifice To kill an animal and offer it as a gift to a g◦

scribe Someone who copies letters and other documents by hand.

viceroy Someone who ac◦ as a deputy to a ruler, taki◦ charge of part of their land◦ A viceroy governed Nubia, territory to the south of Ancient Egypt.

vizier Someone who acts ◦ a deputy to a ruler, taking charge of part of their land◦ Two viziers governed Uppe◦ and Lower Egypt.

Further Information

More Books to Read

cyclopedia of Ancient
ypt
sborne Publishing, 2004)

orge Hart
ewitness: Ancient Egypt
K Children, 2000)

Gill Harvey and Struan Reid
If I Were a Kid in Ancient Egypt
(Cricket Books, 2007)

Fiona Macdonald
Women in Ancient Egypt
(Peter Bedrick, 1999)

John Malam
Ancient Egyptian Jobs
(Heinemann, 2002)

Stewart Ross
Ancient Egypt
(Hodder Wayland, 2006)

Web Sites

Due to the changing nature of Internet links, PowerKids Press has developed an online list of Web Sites related to the subject of this book. This site is regularly updated. Please use this link to access this list: www.powerkidslinks.com/hpl/egypt

INDEX

Numbers in **bold** indicate pictures.